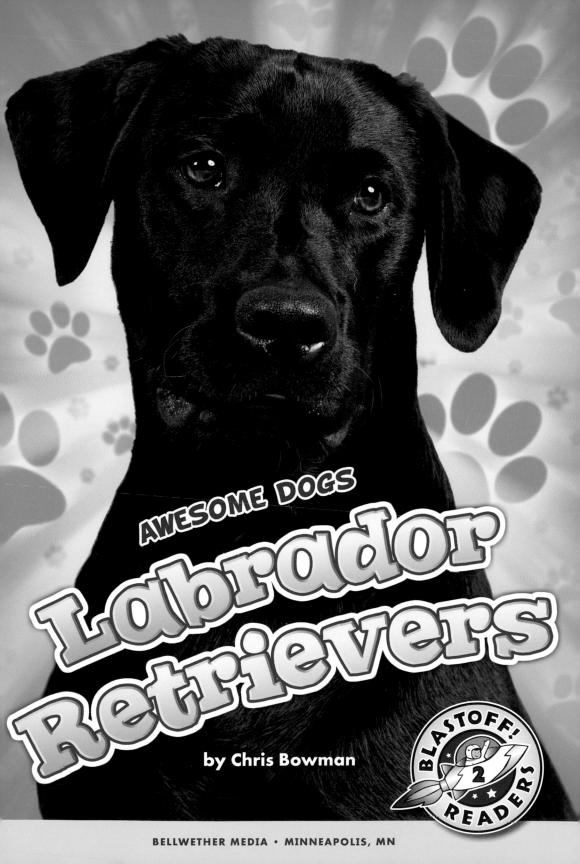

AWESOME DOGS

Labrador Retrievers

by Chris Bowman

BLASTOFF!
2
READERS

BELLWETHER MEDIA • MINNEAPOLIS, MN

Note to Librarians, Teachers, and Parents:

Blastoff! Readers are carefully developed by literacy experts and combine standards-based content with developmentally appropriate text.

Level 1 provides the most support through repetition of high-frequency words, light text, predictable sentence patterns, and strong visual support.

Level 2 offers early readers a bit more challenge through varied simple sentences, increased text load, and less repetition of high-frequency words.

Level 3 advances early-fluent readers toward fluency through increased text and concept load, less reliance on visuals, longer sentences, and more literary language.

Level 4 builds reading stamina by providing more text per page, increased use of punctuation, greater variation in sentence patterns, and increasingly challenging vocabulary.

Level 5 encourages children to move from "learning to read" to "reading to learn" by providing even more text, varied writing styles, and less familiar topics.

Whichever book is right for your reader, Blastoff! Readers are the perfect books to build confidence and encourage a love of reading that will last a lifetime!

This edition first published in 2016 by Bellwether Media, Inc.

No part of this publication may be reproduced in whole or in part without written permission of the publisher. For information regarding permission, write to Bellwether Media, Inc., Attention: Permissions Department, 5357 Penn Avenue South, Minneapolis, MN 55419.

Library of Congress Cataloging-in-Publication Data

Bowman, Chris, 1990- author.
  Labrador Retrievers / by Chris Bowman.
    pages cm. – (Blastoff! Readers. Awesome Dogs)
  Summary: "Relevant images match informative text in this introduction to Labrador retrievers. Intended for students in kindergarten through third grade"– Provided by publisher.
  Audience: Ages 5-8
  Audience: K to grade 3
  Includes bibliographical references and index.
  ISBN 978-1-62617-242-5 (hardcover: alk. paper)
  1. Labrador retriever–Juvenile literature. 2. Hunting dogs–Juvenile literature. I. Title.
  SF429.L3B68 2016
  636.7527–dc23
                        2015009465

Printed in the United States of America, North Mankato, MN.

Table of Contents

What Are Labrador Retrievers?

Labrador retrievers are the most popular dog **breed** in the United States. They are loved for their active and friendly nature.

Their name is often shortened
to Labs.

Labs are strong,
medium-sized dogs.

They have wide heads
and friendly faces.

These dogs have thick **coats**.
Their fur can be black, yellow,
or chocolate in color.

Labrador Retriever Coats

black   yellow   chocolate

Their top layer of fur is short and straight.

A soft **undercoat** keeps Labs
warm and dry in water.

Labrador Retriever Profile

thick tail

wide head —

webbed paws

Life Span: 12 to 14 years

Trainability:

1   2   3   4   5   6

Hardest to train   Easiest to train

Webbed paws and thick tails help them swim.

History of Labrador Retrievers

Labrador retrievers are from Newfoundland, Canada. They helped fishermen in the 1700s.

Newfoundland

Canada

N
W E
S

Newfoundland dog

They most likely came from a mix of small water dogs and Newfoundland dogs.

Then British visitors took Labs home. The dogs became favorite hunting partners of an English **noble**.

His family continued **breeding** them to fetch birds.

Soon, Labs were brought to the United States.

The **American Kennel Club** now places them in the **Sporting Group**.

Active and Loving

Labrador retrievers need a lot of exercise. These **athletic** dogs make great hunting helpers.

Many Labs work with **search and rescue**.

Labs like to please. This makes them great **service dogs**. It also makes them favorite family pets.

Labrador retrievers do well in many different jobs!

Glossary

American Kennel Club—an organization that keeps track of dog breeds in the United States

athletic—being strong, fit, and active

breed—a type of dog

breeding—purposely mating two dogs to make puppies with certain qualities

coats—the hair or fur covering some animals

noble—a member of the British upper class

search and rescue—teams that look for and help people in danger

service dogs—dogs trained to help people who have special needs perform daily tasks

Sporting Group—a group of dog breeds that are active and need regular exercise

undercoat—a layer of short, soft hair or fur some dog breeds have to keep warm

webbed paws—paws with thin skin that connects the toes

To Learn More

AT THE LIBRARY
Barnes, Nico. *Labrador Retrievers*. Minneapolis,
Minn.: Abdo Kids, 2015.

Bodden, Valerie. *Retrievers*. Mankato, Minn.:
Creative Education, 2014.

Landau, Elaine. *Labrador Retrievers Are the Best!*
Minneapolis, Minn.: Lerner Publications, 2010.

ON THE WEB
Learning more about
Labrador retrievers
is as easy as 1, 2, 3.

1. Go to www.factsurfer.com.

2. Enter "Labrador retrievers" into the search box.

3. Click the "Surf" button and you will see a
   list of related web sites.

With factsurfer.com, finding more
information is just a click away.

Index

The images in this book are reproduced through the courtesy of: Ysbrand Cosijn, front cover, p. 9 (right); Susan Schmitz, p. 4; Capture Light, p. 5; Baevskiy Dmitry, p. 6; Eric Isselee, pp. 7, 9 (left, center), 16; Peter Faber/ Glow Images, pp. 8-9; Michael Krabs/ imagebroker/ Age Fotostock, p. 10; ArtSilense, p. 11; Viorel Sima, p. 12; Utekhina Anna, p. 13; Amoret Tanner/ Alamy, p. 14; Linn Currie, p. 15; Juniors/ SuperStock, p. 17; Roland Ijdema, p. 18; blickwinkel/ Alamy, p. 19; National Geographic Image Collection/ Alamy, p. 20; Zuma Press/ Alamy, p. 21.